Super Explorers

EXPLORING SPACE

Tamara Hartson

Contents

What is Space?

Space is also sometimes called outer space. It is the dark and starry place beyond Earth. The planet Earth is in space, just like the Sun and the Moon.

Even though space looks like it is full of stars, it is really quite empty. The distance between stars in space is very far.

Many interesting things are found in space, such as planets, stars, galaxies, nebulas, asteroids and comets. Astronauts explore space using spacecraft and robots. Astronomers explore space using telescopes and satellites that send information back to Earth.

What is a Planet?

A planet is a spherical (round) body that orbits (circles) a star. Planets can be made of rock, gas or ice. Rocky planets are usually smaller than gas or gas and ice planets. Earth is a rocky planet.

A rogue planet is one that does not orbit a star. Rogue planets circle around the center of the galaxy instead.

What is a Moon?

A **moon** is a rocky or icy body that orbits a planet. Some moons are spherical, but others are irregular. Moons are also called **natural satellites**.

Our Solar System has 8 planets that orbit the Sun. Some planets have moons. Earth has one moon, and Jupiter has 79!

The eight planets in order: Mercury, Venus, Earth, Mars, Jupiter, Saturn, Uranus and Neptune.

Pluto was once thought to be a planet, but it is now called a dwarf planet, meaning it is too small to be seen as a true planet.

The Sun's gravity is what keeps all the planets circling around it.

Solar System

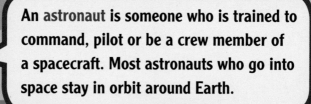

An **astronaut** is someone who is trained to command, pilot or be a crew member of a spacecraft. Most astronauts who go into space stay in orbit around Earth.

Astronaut **Neil Armstrong was** the first person to walk on the Moon. He stepped onto the Moon on July 21, 1969.

As of summer 2021, 574 astronauts from 41 countries have been in space. Some astronauts spend a few months in space. They do research on the International Space Station (ISS) and do work on satellites.

Astronauts

International Space Station

The International Space Station (ISS) is a research station in space. Astronauts from many countries travel to the ISS in spacecraft. The United States, Russia, Europe, Japan and Canada all helped to build the station.

The crew of the ISS do not need spacesuits while they are inside the space station.

The ISS has 16 large solar panels to generate energy for electricity. Each solar panel is about the size of the land needed for a house with a front and back yard.

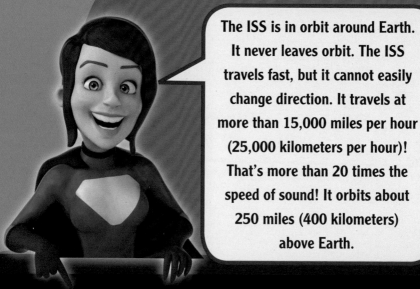

The ISS is in orbit around Earth. It never leaves orbit. The ISS travels fast, but it cannot easily change direction. It travels at more than 15,000 miles per hour (25,000 kilometers per hour)! That's more than 20 times the speed of sound! It orbits about 250 miles (400 kilometers) above Earth.

Where is the ISS?

Although it sounds like the ISS is really far away from Earth, it isn't far at all. Sailors on the ocean can be as far as 1600 miles (2593 kilometers) from land, while astronauts on the ISS are only 250 miles (400 kilometers) away. Working in space is much more dangerous than working on an ocean-going ship!

The astronauts aboard the ISS always stay in communication with their Flight Control Team at National Aeronautics and Space Administration (NASA).

A Flight Control Team supervises the ISS and its crew from NASA's Johnson Space Center in Houston.

Communication

The Flight Control Team is made up of various kinds of engineers who monitor the systems on the spacecraft. The Flight Director is in constant communication with the ISS. A Flight Surgeon monitors the health of each crew member.

Tiangong Space Station

Tiangong Space Station is currently being built by China Manned Space Agency (CMSA). *Tiangong* means Palace in the Sky in Chinese.

The goals of this space station are to:
- conduct scientific experiments
- develop new spacecraft
- create better fuels and fuelling technology
- aid in deep space exploration.

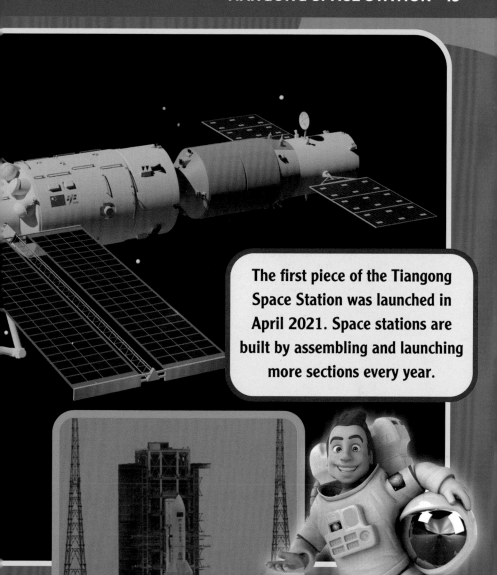

The first piece of the Tiangong Space Station was launched in April 2021. Space stations are built by assembling and launching more sections every year.

Lunar Gateway

The Lunar Gateway (or Gateway, for short), is a small space station still in the planning stage. NASA, European Space Agency (ESA), Japan Aerospace Exploration Agency (JAXA) and Canadian Space Agency (CSA) are all working together to build this station.

Gateway will be a laboratory and hub to support manned missions to the Moon, Mars and maybe even deeper into our Solar System.

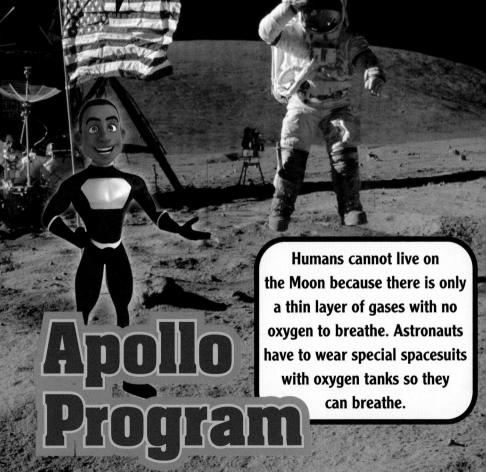

People have made 9 trips to the Moon. Each trip was called an Apollo Mission. In total, 12 astronauts have walked on the Moon. The Moon has less gravity than Earth, so walking on the Moon is like bouncing very slowly. On the moon, you could easily jump as high as a 6-storey buiding!

Humans cannot live on the Moon because there is only a thin layer of gases with no oxygen to breathe. Astronauts have to wear special spacesuits with oxygen tanks so they can breathe.

Apollo Program

The **Lunar Roving Vehicle** is a special type of car that astronauts took to the Moon. Three different cars were made and taken to the Moon. All three are still there!

This footprint on the surface of the Moon was made by Astronaut Buzz Aldrin. It will stay there for a long, long time because there is no wind or water on the Moon to move the dust around.

Artemis Program

No one has been back to the Moon since the last Apollo Mission in December 1972. A new program, named Artemis after the Greek Goddess of the Moon, hopes to take people back to the Moon by 2025.

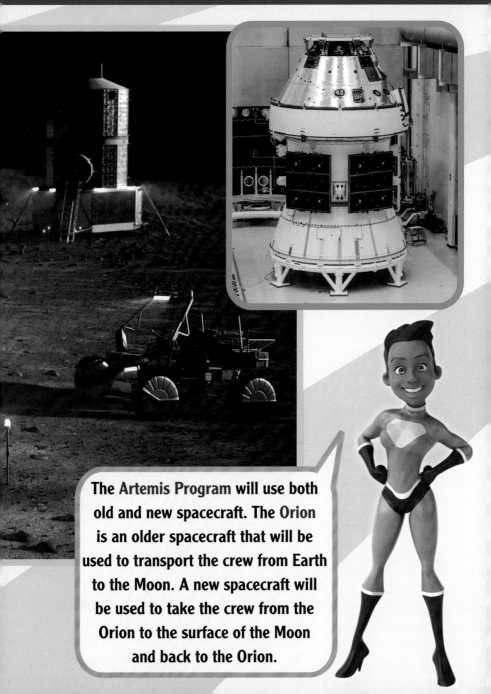

The Artemis Program will use both old and new spacecraft. The Orion is an older spacecraft that will be used to transport the crew from Earth to the Moon. A new spacecraft will be used to take the crew from the Orion to the surface of the Moon and back to the Orion.

People have never been to Mars. Scientists are planning to build special spacecraft that one day may take astronauts to Mars.

Scientists have sent 6 rovers to Mars. Three of them are still sending information and photos back to Earth.

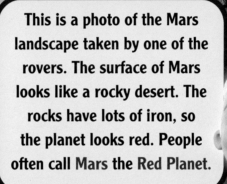

This is a photo of the Mars landscape taken by one of the rovers. The surface of Mars looks like a rocky desert. The rocks have lots of iron, so the planet looks red. People often call Mars the Red Planet.

Mars Missions

Private Space Exploration

In the last 20 years, space flight has become popular with private companies. At one time, only government organizations, like NASA, explored space.

Two of the most famous companies are Blue Origin, founded by Jeff Bezos, and SpaceX, founded by Elon Musk. SpaceX's Falcon rockets have taken off and landed more than 100 times!

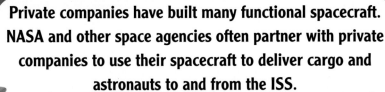

Private companies have built many functional spacecraft. NASA and other space agencies often partner with private companies to use their spacecraft to deliver cargo and astronauts to and from the ISS.

Blue Origin's spacecraft *New Shepard* has taken private citizens into near-Earth orbit. In October 2021, William Shatner, who played Captain Kirk in *Star Trek*, went into space aboard the second crewed flight of the *New Shepard*.

Astronomers today use special computers and telescopes to learn about space.

People used to think Earth was the center of the universe. Nicolaus Copernicus was one of the first astronomers to say that Earth revolves around the Sun.

A long time ago, Galileo Galilei used his telescope to see the movement of the planets. He also discovered the 4 largest moons of Jupiter.

Astronomers

Observatories

Observatories are special buildings for telescopes where astronomers can study space. Observatories are built in places far away from city lights, like on mountaintops.

Some observatories are actually built into airplanes or balloons! These are called airborne observatories. Being in the air allows the telescopes to be used above the clouds, far away from light sources.

Some observatories have arrays of radio telescopes that look like large dishes or bowls. They collect radio signals from space. All the radio signals scientists have detected so far have come from natural objects and events in space.

Images from the Hubble Telescope are the best pictures we have of the amazing things in space.

Helix Nebula

Whirpool Galaxy

Crab Nebula

Eagle Nebula

Hubble Telescope

The Hubble Telescope is a special telescope because it was made to work in space. It has been in orbit around Earth since it was launched in 1990. It takes photos of planets, stars, galaxies and nebulas.

James Webb Space Telescope

This telescope can see objects 100 times fainter than the Hubble can. It can even give atmospheric details of distant, possibly habitable planets beyond our Solar System.

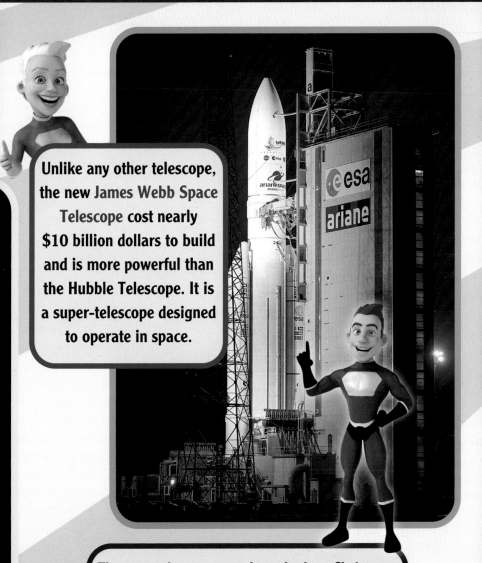

Unlike any other telescope, the new James Webb Space Telescope cost nearly $10 billion dollars to build and is more powerful than the Hubble Telescope. It is a super-telescope designed to operate in space.

The new telescope was launched on Christmas Day 2021. Scientists hope it will provide detailed images of distant objects and events in space for 5 to 10 years.

A star is a hot sphere of glowing gas. Stars produce heat, light and energy. We only see stars at night because the light of the Sun prevents us from seeing them during the day.

Stars

The Sun is the closest star to Earth. Light from the Sun takes 8 minutes and 20 seconds to reach Earth. The next closest star to us is called Proxima Centauri. Light from this star takes more than 4 years to reach Earth!

This collection of stars is nicknamed a nursery because every year a new star is born here.
There are more stars in the universe than there are grains of sand on Earth. That's a lot of stars!

The smallest and dimmest stars are tiny red dwarfs. Astronomers have found a red dwarf star that is only a bit bigger than Jupiter.

Red Dwarfs & Supergiants

The largest stars are called supergiants. Some supergiants look blue, and others may look red. These huge stars are also very bright.

If the largest supergiant replaced our sun, it would reach almost all the way to Saturn.

When a supergiant star is at the end of its life, it explodes. The explosion is called a supernova. This purple cloud is left over from a massive supernova.

This supernova explosion is extremely powerful. Scientists are watching as the cloud gets bigger.

Supernovas

Galaxies are large groups of stars held together by gravity. Sometimes galaxies have different shapes, like spirals, because of the way the stars rotate around the center. Our Solar System is in a spiral galaxy called the Milky Way.

Star clusters are smaller than galaxies and have fewer stars. This is a photo of the Messier 92 star cluster.

Sometimes galaxies form groups. Seyfert's Sextet is a group of 6 different galaxies. Galaxies in clusters are held together by gravity. Superclusters can contain thousands of galaxies!

Galaxies & Star Clusters

Black Holes

A black hole is a part of space with very strong gravity. The pull of gravity in a black hole is so powerful, all light and matter disappear into it.

The bright stars at the center of this large, spiral galaxy hide a massive black hole. Our galaxy, the Milky Way, also has a black hole at its center.

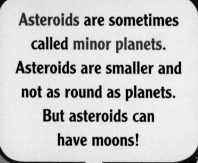

Asteroids are sometimes called minor planets. Asteroids are smaller and not as round as planets. But asteroids can have moons!

Meteoroids are similar to asteroids but they are much smaller—many are not as wide as you are tall.

Asteroids and meteoroides are made of rock and minerals. They have unusual shapes. Like planets, asteroids orbit the Sun. There are more than one million asteroids in our Solar System.

Asteroids & Meteoroids

DART Mission

If a meteoroid or asteroid passes through the Earth's atmosphere and doesn't completely burn up, the remaining part of it may hit the ground. Once a meteoroid hits the ground, it is called a meteorite. A large meteorite impact is responsible for the dinosaurs dying out.

DART stands for Double Asteroid Redirection Test. It could become part of Earth's planetary defense program.

NASA has recently launched a spacecraft designed to smash into an asteroid to try and alter its course. If it works, scientists and engineers will build more spacecraft to use if an asteroid is on a collision course with Earth.

Comets

Comets are like big, dirty snowballs. They are mostly made of ice, dust and rock. The tail of a comet is made of dust and gas.

More than 5000 comets orbit the Sun in our Solar System. Some comets pass close to Earth as they orbit the sun. Other comets pass by Earth every 20 years. Others may take hundreds or even thousands of years to return.

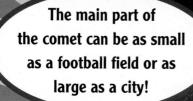

The main part of the comet can be as small as a football field or as large as a city!

When a comet is close to Earth, we can see it in the night sky. Halley's Comet passes by Earth every 75 years.

Nebulas are large clouds of dust and gases in space. Sometimes so much gas and dust collects in a nebula that stars can form inside the clouds.

Nebulas

The Cat's Eye Nebula is a gas nebula.

Some nebulas have two wings. These types of nebula are formed by dying red giant stars.

Sun

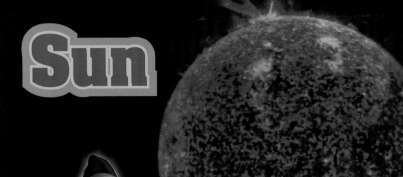

The Sun is the center of our Solar System. It is also called Sol. The Sun produces light, heat and energy. Without the Sun, life could not survive on Earth.

Even though we think of stars as tiny, bright dots in the night sky, the Sun is actually the closest star to Earth.

Our Sun is an average yellow star. There are trillions of other stars just like it in the universe. Many of these other stars may even have planets like Earth orbiting them.

In 2018, NASA launched the Parker Solar Probe. In November 2021, it flew into the outer atmosphere of the Sun, sending back data about its flow of energy and magnetic field.

Mercury

LOCATION: First planet from the sun

TIME TO CIRCLE THE SUN: 88 days

NUMBER OF MOONS: 0

CAN HUMANS LIVE HERE: No

TIME FOR SUNLIGHT TO REACH THE PLANET: 3.2 minutes

DISTANCE FROM THE SUN: 35 million miles (average)
57 million kilometers (average)

AVERAGE SURFACE TEMPERATURE: Hot! (243 °F) (117 °C)

GRAVITY: Less than Earth. 100 pounds (45 kilograms) on Earth is 38 pounds (17 kilograms) on Mercury.

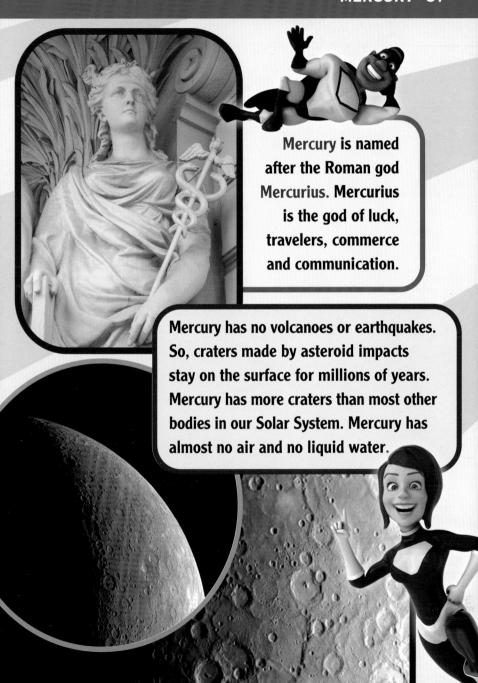

Mercury is named after the Roman god Mercurius. Mercurius is the god of luck, travelers, commerce and communication.

Mercury has no volcanoes or earthquakes. So, craters made by asteroid impacts stay on the surface for millions of years. Mercury has more craters than most other bodies in our Solar System. Mercury has almost no air and no liquid water.

Venus

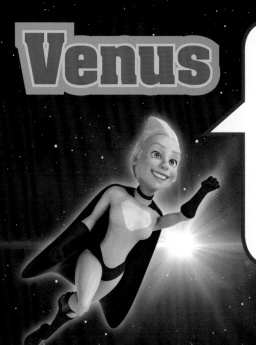

Venus is the planet most similar in size to Earth. It is very different in other ways. The temperature is 30 times hotter than Earth, and the clouds are made of acid droplets instead of rain!

LOCATION: Second planet from the sun
TIME TO CIRCLE THE SUN: 224.7 days
NUMBER OF MOONS: 0
CAN HUMANS LIVE HERE: No
TIME FOR SUNLIGHT TO REACH THE PLANET: 6 minutes
DISTANCE FROM THE SUN: 67 million miles (average)
                      108 million kilometers (average)
AVERAGE SURFACE TEMPERATURE: Very hot! (863 °F) (462 °C)
GRAVITY: Similar to Earth. 100 pounds (45 kilograms)
    on Earth is 91 pounds (41 kilograms) on Venus.

Earth

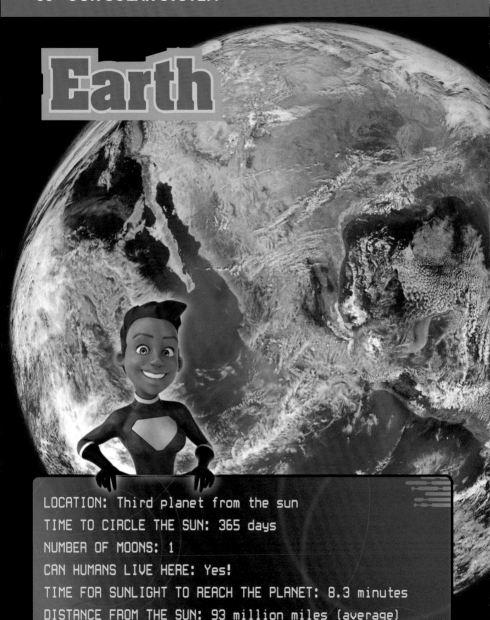

LOCATION: Third planet from the sun

TIME TO CIRCLE THE SUN: 365 days

NUMBER OF MOONS: 1

CAN HUMANS LIVE HERE: Yes!

TIME FOR SUNLIGHT TO REACH THE PLANET: 8.3 minutes

DISTANCE FROM THE SUN: 93 million miles (average)
150 million kilometers (average)

AVERAGE SURFACE TEMPERATURE: Perfect! (59 °F) (15 °C)

Our Home

Earth is the fifth largest planet in our Solar System. Most of the Earth is covered by oceans. More than 8 million kinds of life live on Earth, including about 7 billion humans.

At night, city lights shine brightly and are visible from space. These night lights are all around the world where people live in large numbers.

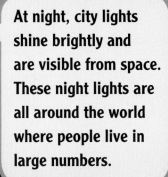

Earth has one moon, called Luna. Our Moon is large and easy to see from Earth. The rise and fall of ocean tides on Earth are caused by the gravity of our Moon.

The Moon even has mountains, but they look very different from the mountains on Earth!

Earth's Moon

The surface of the Moon is covered in craters. These craters are formed when asteroids hit the Moon's surface.

Mars

Mars has polar ice caps just like Earth.

LOCATION: Fourth planet from the sun

TIME TO CIRCLE THE SUN: 686.9 days

NUMBER OF MOONS: 2

CAN HUMANS LIVE HERE: No

TIME FOR SUNLIGHT TO REACH THE PLANET: 12.6 minutes

DISTANCE FROM THE SUN: 141 million miles (average)
228 million kilometers (average)

AVERAGE SURFACE TEMPERATURE: Cold! (-81 °F) (-63 °C)

GRAVITY: Less than Earth. 100 pounds (45 kilograms) on Earth is 38 pounds (17 kilograms) on Mars.

Mars is the fourth planet in our Solar System. Mars is a rocky planet. It is different from Earth because it is smaller and doesn't have oceans. The air on Mars is thin and has little oxygen.

The surface of Mars looks like a rocky desert. The rocks have lots of iron, so the planet looks red. People often call Mars the Red Planet.

Moons of Mars

Mars has two moons. They are named Phobos and Deimos. Phobos is the larger moon, and It Is closer to Mars. The closer a satellite is to a planet, the faster it has to move to stay in orbit. Phobos moves so fast that it rises and sets twice each Martian day.

Deimos

Phobos

At its longest, Phobos is only
17 miles (27 kilometers) long.
Deimos is about half that size.
The two moons are named after
Greek gods that are twin brothers.

#

Jupiter is the largest planet in our Solar System. The Romans named this planet after their god Jupiter, god of the sky. Jupiter is easy to see in the sky. It is the third brightest object after the Moon and Venus.

LOCATION: Fifth planet from the sun

TIME TO CIRCLE THE SUN: Almost 12 years

NUMBER OF MOONS: 79

CAN HUMANS LIVE HERE: No

TIME FOR SUNLIGHT TO REACH THE PLANET: 43.2 minutes

DISTANCE FROM THE SUN: 141 million miles (average)
                      228 million kilometers (average)

AVERAGE SURFACE TEMPERATURE: Very cold! (-234 °F) (-148 °C)

GRAVITY: More than Earth. 100 pounds (45 kilograms)
    on Earth is 253 pounds (115 kilograms) on Jupiter.

Jupiter has 79 moons! Most of Jupiter's moons have irregular shapes and are small. The four main moons are large and spherical. They are called the Galilean Moons.

Jupiter's Great Red Spot is a massive, turning storm that has existed for several hundred years!

This is the view of Jupiter's south pole. It is many different images pieced together and is the most detailed view of Jupiter's southern region. The images were taken by the space probe *Cassini* in the year 2000.

Did you know that Jupiter has rings? Unlike the rings of Saturn, Jupiter's rings are mostly made of dust and are faint. They are only visible with powerful telescopes or from space probes sent to Jupiter. There are 4 rings: Halo, Main Ring, Amalthea Gossamer Ring and Thebe Gossamer Ring.

Halo

Main Ring

Amalthea Gossamer Ring

Thebe Gossamer Ring

Io

Europa

Ganymede

Callisto

A long time ago, Galileo Galilei used his telescope to see the movement of the planets. He also discovered the 4 largest moons of Jupiter. They are called the Galilean Moons.

Galilean Moons

This is a painting of what scientists believe it would be like to stand on Europa, the smallest of the Galilean moons. Europa may have a vast ocean under its crust. Researchers believe it would be a good place to look for extraterrestrial life, such as single-celled organisms.

Saturn

LOCATION: Sixth planet from the sun

TIME TO CIRCLE THE SUN: Almost 30 years

NUMBER OF MOONS: 62

CAN HUMANS LIVE HERE: No

TIME FOR SUNLIGHT TO REACH THE PLANET: 1.3 hours

DISTANCE FROM THE SUN: 886 million miles (average)
          1.4 billion kilometers (average)

AVERAGE SURFACE TEMPERATURE: Very cold! (-288 °F) (-178 °C)

GRAVITY: Similar to Earth. 100 pounds (45 kilograms)
    on Earth is 107 pounds (49 kilograms) on Saturn.

Saturn is the most recognizable of all the planets because of its rings.

Saturn spins so fast that it actually has a distorted shape. Instead of being truly spherical, it bulges around the middle. Saturn weighs very little for its size. If there were a lake big enough, Saturn would float!

Janus

Mimas

Titan

Saturn's moons vary greatly in size and shape. Titan is Saturn's largest moon, and the second largest moon in our Solar System. This photograph of Saturn shows 6 of Saturn's 62 moons.

Saturn's Moons

Pandora

Enceladus

Epimetheus

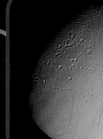

Titan

Epimetheus

Rings

Titan

Titan is a large moon. It is bigger than the planet Mercury! Here is Titan behind the rings of Saturn and the much smaller moon Epimetheus.

The space probe *Huygens* landed on Titan and took this picture of the surface.

Titan is the only moon in our Solar System that has an atmosphere. Many scientists want to send more probes to Titan because they think single-celled organisms might be able to live there. But so far, scientists have found no evidence of life on Titan.

High-Pressure Ice

Liquid Water Ocean

Ice

Rocky Surface

Solid Core

Atmosphere

Uranus

Uranus is unusual because the planet, its rings and its moons appear to be tilted sideways! Scientists think that when the planet and moons were nearly formed, it collided with several large objects, causing everything to tilt.

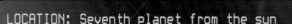

LOCATION: Seventh planet from the sun

TIME TO CIRCLE THE SUN: About 84 years

NUMBER OF MOONS: 27

CAN HUMANS LIVE HERE: No

TIME FOR SUNLIGHT TO REACH THE PLANET: 2.6 hours

DISTANCE FROM THE SUN: 1.8 billion miles (average)
2.8 billion kilometers (average)

AVERAGE SURFACE TEMPERATURE: Very cold! (-357 °F) (-216 °C)

GRAVITY: Similar to Earth. 100 pounds (45 kilograms) on Earth is 91 pounds (41 kilograms) on Uranus.

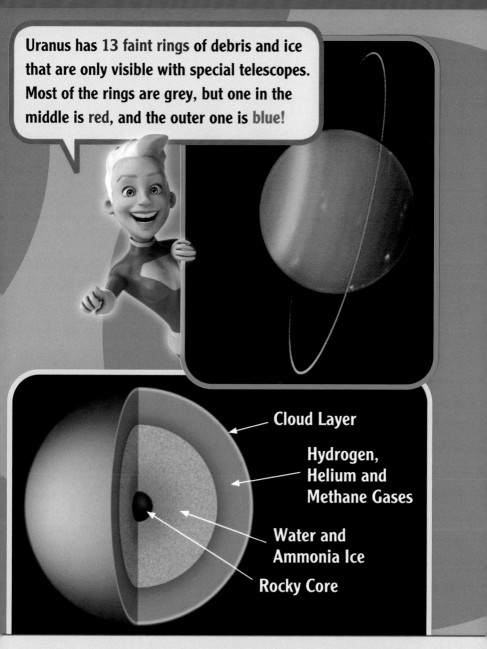

Uranus has **13 faint rings** of debris and ice that are only visible with special telescopes. Most of the rings are grey, but one in the middle is red, and the outer one is blue!

Cloud Layer

Hydrogen, Helium and Methane Gases

Water and Ammonia Ice

Rocky Core

Uranus is an ice giant. It has more ice than a gas giant.

Moons of Uranus

Uranus has **27 moons**, all of which were named after characters in the works of Shakespeare. This image of Uranus shows several of its moons.

Umbriel

Titania

Miranda

Ariel

Oberon

These are the 5 main moons of Uranus. They are all made of about equal parts rock and ice. Miranda has the most uneven surface of any object in our Solar System!

Neptune

Neptune is the farthest planet from the sun. It is named after the Roman god of the sea. Neptune is the only planet in our Solar System that wasn't discovered by seeing it. An astronomer predicted that a big planet must exist beyond Uranus because of how Uranus's orbit varied. Twenty years later, in 1846, astronomers found Neptune using a telescope.

LOCATION: Eighth planet from the sun

TIME TO CIRCLE THE SUN: Almost 165 years

NUMBER OF MOONS: 14

CAN HUMANS LIVE HERE: No

TIME FOR SUNLIGHT TO REACH THE PLANET: 4.1 hours

DISTANCE FROM THE SUN: 2.8 billion miles (average)
4.5 billion kilometers (average)

AVERAGE SURFACE TEMPERATURE: VERY COLD! (-357 °F) (-216 °C)

GRAVITY: Similar to Earth. 100 pounds (45 kilograms)
on Earth is 91 pounds (41 kilograms) on Uranus.

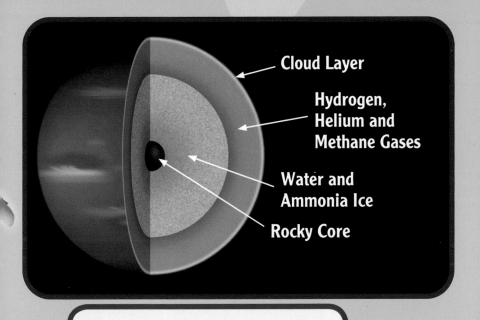

Cloud Layer

Hydrogen,
Helium and
Methane Gases

Water and
Ammonia Ice

Rocky Core

Like Uranus, Neptune is an ice giant. The cloud layer has a large dark spot the size of Earth. This spot is a big storm just like the red spot on Jupiter.

Neptune's Moons & Rings

This photo of Neptune shows 3 of its moons!

Proteus

Despina

Larissa

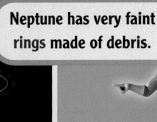

Neptune has very faint rings made of debris.

Triton is Neptune's only moon big enough to be a sphere. It has the texture of a cantaloupe! Below is a painting of the surface of Triton with Neptune and the Sun in the sky.

Triton

Dwarf planets are similar to planets. They are round and orbit the Sun. Unlike true planets, dwarf planets are quite small and share their orbit with asteroids. This is a photo of Pluto. Although it was once called a planet, it is now considered a dwarf planet. Pluto has 5 moons!

Pluto

Ceres

Ceres is a dwarf planet between Mars and Jupiter. It orbits the Sun along with millions of asteroids. Together, they are called the Asteroid Belt. Ceres is the only dwarf planet in the Asteroid Belt.

So far, there are only 5 official dwarf planets, Ceres, Pluto, Eris, Makemake and Haumea. Several round objects close to Pluto may soon be classified as dwarf planets. Astronomers think there may be hundreds of dwarf planets still to be found in our Solar System.

Eris

Dwarf Planets

Pluto's moon, Charon, is such a large moon that some astronomers call the two a double-dwarf planet.

Charon is a little more than half the size of Pluto, and it is made of ice and rock. This is a painting of the surface of Charon, with Pluto as a crescent and the Sun in the distance.

Dysnomia is Eris's only moon. In Greek mythology, Dysnomia is the daughter of the Greek goddess Eris. Detecting moons of dwarf planets is hard because they are so small. Astronomers think that they will find more dwarf planets and moons as telescopes become more powerful.

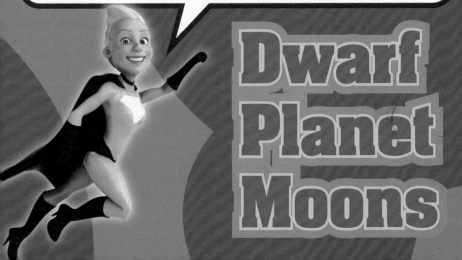

Dwarf Planet Moons

An exoplanet is any planet outside of our Solar System. The first confirmed discovery of an exoplanet was in 1992. Now astronomers have detected several thousand exoplanets. Even though we don't have photographs of exoplanets, artists have painted pictures of what we imagine they look like.

Exoplanets

In the search for exoplanets, astronomers look for planets in the habitable zone—the distance from a star that allows for liquid water. We currently know of nearly 5000 exoplanets, and many of these are in the habitable zone of their stars.

Life Beyond Earth?

When people think of alien life, they usually imagine strange green creatures. However, the most likely life beyond Earth will be single-celled creatures. Astronomers are always looking for radio signals, one of the likely signs of intelligent life.

Geysers on Enceladus

The most likely place to find extraterrestrial life might be Enceladus, one of Saturn's moons. It has geysers of ice, meaning that liquid water may be found under the surface. Life as we know it needs water to survive.

The Publisher: Super Explorers is an imprint of Blue Bike Books

Library and Archives Canada Cataloguing in Publication

Title: Exploring space / Tamara Hartson.

Names: Hartson, Tamara, 1974– author.

Identifiers: Canadiana (print) 20220142610 | Canadiana (ebook) 20220142629 | ISBN

9781989209165 (softcover) | ISBN 9781989209172 (PDF)

Subjects: LCSH: Outer space—Exploration—Juvenile literature. | LCSH: Interplanetary voyages

—Juvenile literature. | LCSH: Astronomy—Juvenile literature. | LCSH: Solar system—Juvenile

literature.

Classification: LCC TL793 .H35 2022 | DDC j629.45—dc23

Front cover credit: NASA

Back cover credits: NASA.

Photo Credits: All photos are courtesy of NASA or ESA/ESO except for the following: Tamara Hartson 54b, Lawrence Sromovsky, W.W. Keck Observatory 81b. From Wikimedia: China News Service 19b, Alan L 32a, Shujianyang 18-19, Kelvinsong 78a. From Thinkstock Photos: RomoloTavani 6-7, Sebastian Kaulitzki 9, Photos.com 30b, valeriopardi 51b, shelma1 54a, themotioncloud 58-59, Stockbyte 63b. From Getty Images: Naeblys 29b.

Superhero Illustrations: julos/Thinkstock.

Produced with the assistance of the Government of Alberta.

Alberta
Government

We acknowledge the financial support of the Government of Canada.
Nous reconnaissons l'appui financier du gouvernement du Canada.

Funded by the Government of Canada
Financé par le gouvernement du Canada

Canadä

Printed in China

PC: 38-1